Jane Austen

by Victor Lucas

Born in the small village of Steventon in Hampshire on 16 December 1775, Jane Austen was the seventh of the eight children of a country parson. It was a time of change. Across the Atlantic the American colonists were locked with the British in their struggle for independence. The Industrial Revolution had not yet arrived but it was on its way. She was 13 years old when the French Revolution broke out, and for most of her adult life, while she wrote her novels in the peaceful intervals of a busy domestic life, England was at war with France.

There is something in the story of Jane Austen's life, and in what she wrote, which opens windows for all her readers, gives men a deeper understanding of the nature of women, and provides both men and women with standards of honesty by which to live their lives. The six completed novels of Jane Austen have never been surpassed for their wit, their style and the truthfulness of their observation. To read and re-read her, to come to value her humanity, her humour, and her insight into human nature, is to gain a good friend for the rest of one's life.

Above: *The Reverend George Austen, Jane's father. At Oxford he was known as 'the handsome Proctor'. Jane spoke of his 'indescribable tenderness as a father' and his 'sweet benevolent smile'.*

Jane Austen's father, the Reverend George Austen, was a classical scholar and a Fellow of his Oxford College, St John's. He was descended from a long line of Kentish yeomen engaged in the wool trade since medieval times. Although his forebears had achieved a degree of prosperity, his parents were very much the poor relations among the Austens, and it was only through the generosity of a wealthy uncle that he was educated at Tonbridge School, from where he went up to Oxford. He became a clergyman, and in 1764 married Cassandra Leigh at Walcot Church in Bath. She came from a more exalted background, numbering among her ancestors Sir Thomas Leigh, a Lord Mayor of London, whose son gave sanctuary to Charles I at the Leigh's family seat at Stoneleigh Abbey in Warwickshire during the Civil War. Both she and her husband were said to be very handsome, and their children inherited something of their parents' good looks.

It was a closely integrated family that grew up in the Rectory at Steventon, a little village not far from Basingstoke in Hampshire. They would always be very supportive of one another and very good friends. The eldest of Jane's brothers was James, who went up to his father's old college and would succeed him as Rector of Steventon. Very little is known of her second brother, George, except that for all his long life of over 70 years he suffered from some extreme mental and physical disorder. Much of the time he was looked after in the village of Monk Sherborne, on the other side of Basingstoke.

No such problem affected any of the other children. The third brother, Edward, was a fortunate young man for whilst still a child he was adopted by the Austens' wealthy but childless kinsman, Thomas Knight of Godmersham Park in Kent, so that he could legally inherit the great house and estate, a stipulation being that he would take the family name of Knight. It was a practical way of ensuring that the money and property remained within the family without becoming the subject of squabbles over inheritance, and gradually the boy was entrusted to the loving care of Thomas Knight and his wife.

The fourth brother, Henry, was a handsome, amiable young man of great charm, adored by his sisters and by almost everybody else, but he changed his mind from time to time about his career. At first he was

Below: *Young Edward being presented by his father to his wealthy relatives, the Knights. He was adopted by them and became their legal heir.*

Above: *Cassandra, Jane's only sister. The two girls had much in common. They enjoyed a close friendship and shared the same sense of humour.*

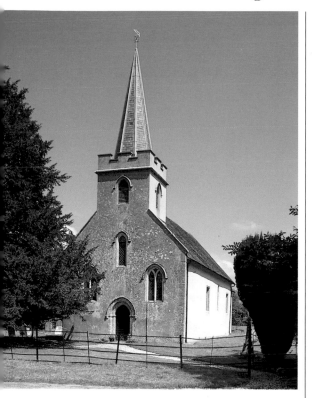

Left: *The Church of St Nicholas, Steventon, stands on a hill apart from the village. Jane's father was rector here for over 30 years, and when he retired in 1800 he was succeeded by his eldest son, James. The weather vane is now in the form of a quill pen, in memory of Jane.*

Her two other brothers, Frank and Charles, were both engaging and lively young boys, who each in turn entered the Navy at the tender age of twelve. They both rose to become admirals, and Frank would acquire a well-merited knighthood on the way. Jane always took a close interest and a great pride in their achievements, and this is reflected in *Persuasion*, in which she writes warmly and knowledgeably of the Navy, and gives sympathetic accounts of Captains Wentworth, Harville and Benwick, and of Admiral Croft. In *Mansfield Park* too she displays much insight into the ways of the service. Her two sailor brothers lived adventurous lives throughout the Napoleonic Wars. Frank took part in Nelson's celebrated sweep to the West Indies in search of the enemy, and later, as Commander of the *Elephant*, he captured an American privateer, the *Swordfish*, in the Baltic. Charles, serving on board the frigate *Unicorn*, was involved in the capture of the French ship

a captain in the Militia, very dashing in his scarlet uniform and always popular with the ladies. After a while he resigned his commission and became a London banker, but when his bank crashed he was ordained as a clergyman, and received from his brother Edward the gift of a clerical living in the country. Jane's only sister, Cassandra, was two years older than Jane and there was a loving relationship between the two girls right from the start which lasted throughout their lives. When Jane arrived, her father wrote in a letter, 'We have now another girl, a present plaything for her sister Cassy, and a future companion. She is to be Jenny...'

Left: *Charles Austen who, like his brother Frank, rose to become an admiral. He would arrive home from voyages abroad laden with presents.*

Below: *The topaz crosses which young Charles sent to his sisters. Jane's cross is the one on the right.*

La Tribune off the Isles of Scilly, after a 200-mile chase, and with his prize money bought two topaz crosses which he sent to his sisters. In *Mansfield Park* Jane uses this incident when the young midshipman William Price buys an amber cross with his prize money, gained under similar circumstances, and sends it to his sister Fanny, for her to wear at her first ball.

Left: *Godmersham Park, near Canterbury, the fine 18th-century house owned by Thomas Knight which would eventually be inherited by Edward.*

Below: *In 1784 Jane and Cassandra were sent to school at the old Abbey in Reading, but it was expensive and they were brought home to be taught by their father.*

The two sisters were inseparable companions. When Cassandra was being sent off to a small private school in Oxford, Jane refused to be left behind. Although only six, she made such a fuss, insisting on not being parted from Cassandra, that she simply had to go too! The school moved to Southampton and the children went with it, but it had to be abruptly disbanded because of an alarming outbreak of what was then called 'the putrid sore throat' – probably diphtheria – a fearsome killer of children. Jane and Cassandra were among those taken ill, and their mother hurriedly travelled to Southampton and took them home to Steventon to be nursed back to health. One of the other mothers, Mrs Austen's sister Jane, on the same errand, caught the infection from her child and died. After they had recovered, the two young girls were sent to a boarding school in the gate-house of the ruins of the old Abbey at Reading. There they were taught by an elderly lady, Mrs Latournelle, who spent much of the time recounting to her charges the gossip of the Green Room at Drury Lane Theatre 50 years before – how the girls enjoyed lessons with Mrs Latournelle! Jane was 11 when they returned to the Rectory, where their further education was now in the hands of their father. The library of the Rectory was filled with books and from an early age Jane became familiar with the plays of Shakespeare and the novels of Fielding, Smollett, Goldsmith and Fanny Burney.

Above: *Jane's childhood copy of* Goody Two-Shoes. *She coloured the illustrations and wrote her name at the top of the page. Like her brothers and sister, Jane read widely from a young age, greatly encouraged by her father.*

The Austen children were voracious readers and very fond of reading aloud to each other. Jane began writing when she was 10 or 11 years old and at 16 she copied out her early works to date in three notebooks; these she called *Volume the First*, *Volume the Second* and *Volume the Third*. They contain sketches, stories, short playlets, a very short comic novel *Love and Freindship* (note her spelling!) and a delightful spoof on that kind of history book which is concerned less with the facts of history than with an historian's prejudice for or against certain historical characters. She called it *The History of England by a Partial Prejudiced and Ignorant Historian*. It begins 'Henry the 4th ascended the throne of England, much to his own satisfaction, in the year 1399.' Already she is doing what she will do many times in her books – giving us, in an economical phrase, and with a twinkle of humour, an insight into the character of the person she is describing.

Her sister illustrated Jane's *History*, depicting the kings and queens of England in the modern dress of her own time. Henry VIII is wearing what appears to be a red nightcap – most appropriate, they felt, for a man who had no fewer than six wedding nights. Queen Elizabeth is seen as a domineering virago (they didn't like Elizabeth!) and Henry VI, who was a very religious king, is in clerical garb, as if he were one of the Reverend George Austen's curates. The child Jane Austen writes, tongue in cheek: 'I suppose you know all about the wars between him and the Duke of York who was of the right side. If you do not you had better read some other History…'

Of Charles I, looking like her young brother of that name, she writes: 'The events of this monarch's reign are too numerous for my pen, and indeed the recital of any events, except what I make myself, is uninteresting to me; my principal reason in undertaking the History of England being to prove the innocence of the Queen of Scotland, which I flatter myself with having effectually done, and to abuse Elizabeth.' Cassandra shows us Mary Queen of Scots as a wronged and beautiful young heroine out of one of the romantic novels of the time, the kind that Jane would have such fun with when she came to write *Northanger Abbey.*

Above and right: *A few of the pages from the young Jane Austen's amusing and 'prejudiced'* History of England, *colourfully illustrated by Cassandra. The two girls spent many hours writing stories and plays and Jane's keen ear for the spoken word derived in part from the family's love of reading to each other.*

ane was an excellent dancer, and as a young girl often went to balls held at the Town Hall in Basingstoke. Dancing was one of the great indoor amusements of the time. There would be a master of ceremonies, whose function it was to effect introductions and open the ball by leading one of the young ladies out on to the floor. Jane danced the stately old-fashioned minuet, and the quadrille, and the spirited Roger de Coverley. The scandalous new dance from the Continent, the waltz, was not acceptable in polite society. It was considered shocking that, whereas in the other dances the lady and gentleman held each other at arm's length throughout, in this daring innovation from Germany they embraced each other, quite close, their arms around each other's waists, looking into each other's eyes, and did not let go until the music stopped – and who knew what that might lead to! Unmarried girls were chaperoned by their older married sisters; in *Pride and Prejudice* Lydia, who at 16 is the flightiest of the Bennet girls, says to her slightly older sisters, 'How I should like to be married

Above: *James, Jane's eldest brother. He followed his father to Oxford where, in his spare time, he edited a periodical and composed poetry.*

Right: *Jane's vivacious cousin, Eliza Hancock, a frequent visitor to Steventon. After the death of her French husband she married Jane's brother Henry, although it is thought that Mrs Austen disapproved.*

> *Men have had every advantage of us in telling their own story. Education has been theirs in so much higher a degree; the pen has been in their hands.*
>
> ANNE ELLIOT, PERSUASION

before any of you, and then *I* would chaperone *you* about to all the balls!'

The real purpose, the real excitement of the ballroom was that it was a place where young people could meet and get to know members of the opposite sex. The ballroom was very much the antechamber to the marriage market – and marriage in Jane Austen's day was virtually the only career open to a respectable woman. To make a good marriage was to acquire security – the prospect of protection by her husband, by her grown-up sons, protection against the rigours of old age – even though any money or property a woman might bring to a marriage would be forfeited to her husband, except in rare circumstances, the moment the ring was slipped upon her finger. Jane lived, as her characters did, in a world in which the rules were made by men for men. In that male-dominated society, to be an unmarried woman was to be at a specific disadvantage. And so it is that one of Jane's themes in her novels – though it is only one among many others – is the manoeuvring by which marriages were arranged among the small landed semi-gentry of the time. Not that Jane approved, any more than Elizabeth Bennet approves in *Pride and Prejudice.*

Her novels are all deeply perceived comedies of manners, unique in their remarkable insight into human nature, especially with regard to relationships between the sexes.

Below: *A delightful turquoise and pearl bracelet which belonged to Jane and which is displayed with the two topaz crosses in Jane Austen's House at Chawton.*

She is better at this than almost any other writer. There is no truer account of sexual chemistry between a man and a woman than that which she portrays, with all its subtle shifts of emphasis, between Elizabeth and Mr Darcy in *Pride and Prejudice*. But there is something deeper still. It is as if there are dark shadows in the garden, outside the candle-lit ballrooms. All those young girls, dancing away to the fiddles, do not stay young for long. All too soon they will be middle-aged, and

Right: *Tom Lefroy, Anne Lefroy's nephew, with whom Jane enjoyed a mild and probably not very serious flirtation when he visited his aunt in 1796.*

Left and below: *The ball-room was a place of great importance and excitement in the social life of a small market town, and Jane and Cassandra attended many dances in nearby Basingstoke. Informal dances were held in their own home and in those of friends. Jane spent many happy evenings at gatherings arranged by her great friend Mrs Anne Lefroy, who lived not far from Steventon and was a generous hostess whose home was very much a social centre.*

then they will be either happy, like Elizabeth Bennet, or unhappy, like Maria Bertram in *Mansfield Park*, depending on whom they marry. For those unfortunate young girls who did not marry and who did not have a loving family around them (or a family who could support them financially), the outlook was bleak.

There was a great deal of real-life drama in the background of Jane's early years. Her vivacious cousin Eliza Hancock, born in India, was the daughter of Jane's aunt, Philadelphia Hancock. Some people hinted at a secret parentage, unsanctified by marriage, and were sure that Eliza was the result of a liaison between Philadelphia and Warren Hastings, Governor-General of India. Eliza was well known to Jane and other members of the family at Steventon, where she encouraged them to take part with her in amateur performances of popular comedies which she had seen played in the theatre at fashionable Tunbridge Wells. Eliza married a French nobleman, becoming Madame la Comtesse de Feuillide. Some years later, the Comte returned alone to Paris to sort out his affairs, the excesses of the Revolution having apparently abated. There he endeavoured to assist a friend, a former mistress it was said, who had been imprisoned, and as a result he was himself arrested and guillotined soon afterwards. Jane was then 19 years old. One can only speculate as to the effect of this nightmare news when it reached the quiet Hampshire rectory.

Another dark shadow fell across her life with the arrest of her aunt Mrs Leigh Perrot, accused

Above: *Mrs Anne Lefroy. Known as 'Madam Lefroy', she was lively and intelligent and a good friend to Jane; the news of her tragic death in 1804 came as a bitter blow.*

of stealing a card of fine French lace from a haberdasher's shop in Bath, a capital charge. A wealthy, rather starchy lady, very conscious of her dignity, Mrs Leigh Perrot was also a woman of principle, and insisted on standing trial to prove her innocence. She spent eight months in custody, living in squalid conditions in the jailer's house in Taunton, awaiting the next Assizes. The crime of which she stood accused was a felony, which meant that, if the verdict went against her, she could be sentenced to hang. The best she could then have hoped for would be that the death sentence be commuted to transportation as a convict to Botany Bay in Australia. Mrs Austen wrote to her, suggesting that Jane and Cassandra should come and live with their aunt in Taunton, to look after her and keep her company. To her great credit Mrs Leigh Perrot declined Mrs Austen's offer. 'I could not endure the thought of two such elegant young ladies being subjected to such scenes.' Subsequent evidence given indicates that the whole episode had been an engineered attempt at petty blackmail by the shopkeeper, which had then misfired because of Mrs Leigh Perrot's determination to clear her name. She was acquitted after a sensational and widely reported trial.

Above: *Mrs Leigh Perrot. An illustration from* The Lady's Magazine, *which contained an account of the trial of Jane's aunt, who was accused of shoplifting.*

In 1800 the Reverend George Austen retired, and moved his family from Steventon to Bath. Jane was devoted to the Rectory, where she had been born and had grown up, and the announcement that they were to leave came as such a shock to her that she collapsed in a faint on the floor of the kitchen. When in *Persuasion* Anne Elliot, also faced with removal to Bath from her family home, speaks of 'dreading the possible heats of September in all the white glare of Bath, and grieving to forgo all the influence, so sweet and so sad, of the autumnal months in the country', the author was recalling something of her own feelings. Bath was in those days newly built, its stone not yet mellowed to the warm golden hue we know today. But arrangements had to be made, and soon Jane is writing light-heartedly enough to Cassandra, 'We plan having a steady Cook, and a young giddy Housemaid, with a sedate middle-aged Man, who is to undertake the double office of Husband to the former and sweetheart to the latter.'

They stayed for a time with the Leigh Perrots. Then, before they settled into a house at 4 Sydney

Right: *Mrs Cassandra Austen, Jane's mother, was proud of her aristocratic connections and her aquiline nose.*

Place, her father took them all off on a seaside holiday. For about six weeks they wandered from one to another of the little watering-places of Hampshire, Devon and Somerset. How charming they must have been in those days, how unspoilt. And it is believed that in one of them – perhaps Sidmouth or Teignmouth – Jane had a brief and tragic romance. She was an attractive woman who had waited for a man she could respect and love and admire. Recollections by one of her nieces of remarks made long afterwards by Cassandra tell us that during this holiday she found just such a man, and that the other members of the family, including Cassandra, nodded and smiled, seeing a love match. He had to leave them for a while but would be rejoining them before the end of their holiday. When the anticipated day of his return came, Jane received instead the shattering news of his sudden death. In what lowness of spirits she must have

Below: *The Royal Crescent in Bath. Jane's years in Bath were not happy ones for her and after the death of her father in 1805 she looked forward to moving away.*

returned to Bath, to live for five very troubled, very difficult years in that beautiful city where everything seemed to go wrong for her.

The following year, Jane and Cassandra were staying with friends at Manydown House in Hampshire, only a few miles from Steventon where brother James was now rector in his father's

> *Any thing is to be preferred or endured rather than marrying without Affection.*
>
> A LETTER DATED 18 NOVEMBER 1814

place. Manydown was a pleasant country house with pretty grounds and gardens, and here one evening, during this visit, Jane received an offer of marriage from the young son of the family. He was a pleasant young man, and she accepted him. She was now 26, which in those days was considered not just the end of youth but the beginning of middle age. The following morning Jane and Cassandra, both in a state of great agitation, arrived at Steventon. They would give James no explanation for their distress but begged him to get the carriage out and drive them back to Bath. Jane had broken off her engagement to a man she liked but realized she did not love.

Below: *Manydown House in Hampshire. It was here that Jane received an offer of marriage and was for a few short hours engaged to the young son of the family, Harris Bigg-Wither.*

Other upsetting experiences came her way at this time, including the tragic death of a particularly close friend, Mrs Anne Lefroy, upon whose judgment and advice she had come to rely, killed by a fall from a horse. And when, at the beginning of 1805, the Reverend George Austen died, it may have been with a sense of relief that Jane, her sister Cassandra, and their mother decided the time had come to leave Bath.

Below: *Frank, later Admiral Sir Francis Austen. He was practical, a good companion and a highly able administrator. He rose to become Admiral of the Fleet.*

Meanwhile Jane's brother Frank had been involved in Kent in organizing the Sea Fencibles, the Home Guard of the day, against the anticipated French invasion but was now stationed in the Naval Dockyard at Portsmouth. He was living in nearby Southampton with his young wife, and he invited his widowed mother and his sisters to come and keep house with them. It must have been pleasant for Jane to be part of a growing family circle again during the next few years. There she completed a novel which she called *Susan* (we know it by its later title *Northanger Abbey*) and she found a London publisher, Crosby, who undertook to bring it out without delay. He paid her £10 for the outright purchase of the book

Above: *Southampton, as it was in 1808. Following their move from Bath in early 1806, Jane and Cassandra and their mother lived with Frank and his wife Mary in a comfortable old-fashioned house with a large garden, in Castle Square.*

and all the future rights in perpetuity. This was very little for such an arrangement, even in those days. The smallness of the sum was partly because it was her first book but also no doubt because she was a woman. However, the prospect of seeing her work in print was exciting and very encouraging. Bitter disappointment followed. Crosby held on to the manuscript but never published it. Months passed into years, and Jane was never to see *Northanger Abbey* in print.

By 1809 Jane's brother Edward, the inheritor of Godmersham Park, owned the Knight properties in Hampshire as well. He was able to place at the disposal of his mother and his sisters the fine, large, handsome cottage known today as Jane Austen's House at Chawton. It has a very pleasant atmosphere still, and Jane was to be very happy there. 'Yes, yes,' she wrote excitedly to Cassandra, 'we will have a pianoforte, as good a one as can be got for 30 guineas, and I will practice country dances that we may have some amusement for our nephews and nieces.'

She was the best aunt that ever there was, and all the children adored her. In the course of her sadly short life she would become the aunt to no less than 24 nephews and nieces. When her niece Caroline herself became an aunt, Jane wrote to her that she was now a person of consequence: 'I have always maintained the importance of aunts.' Caroline, in old age, said that as a very little girl she used to follow Aunt Jane about, very close, wherever she went, in

Left: Edward (Austen) Knight, who provided a home for his mother and sisters at Chawton.

the house and in the garden. 'She seemed to love you, and you loved her in return.'

During these happy days at Chawton, Jane busied herself with gardening, wine making, writing out her music books and helping her mother and sister make a colourful patchwork quilt. It can be seen today on a wall of the cottage.

Left: A fashion print of the time. A loving aunt, Jane sent a 'secret' letter to one of her nieces, 'that little puss Cassie'. Written backwards, it began 'Ym raed Yssac'.

Above: *One of Jane's music books, on view in the house. She ruled the lines and neatly inked in all the notes herself.*

Left: *The drawing room at Chawton. Jane, her mother and sister moved to Chawton Cottage, as it was then called, in the summer of 1809. The piano is probably very like the one she bought to entertain their many young visitors.*

Left: *The Pump Room was very much the centre of the social world in Bath. In* Northanger Abbey *Jane tells us something of it: 'Mr Allen, after drinking his glass of water, joined some gentlemen to talk over the politics of the day and compare the accounts of their newspapers; and the ladies walked about together, noticing every new face and almost every new bonnet in the room.'*

In 1811 came the turning point in Jane's life – the publication of *Sense and Sensibility*, the first of the books in which she presented so true and so entertaining an account of the life she knew in and around the small country towns of the south of England. During the period of waiting between acceptance and publication this 35-year-old spinster wrote of the book, 'I am never too busy to think of S&S. I can no more forget it, than a mother can forget her sucking child.' *Sense and Sensibility* sold well but her name did not appear upon it. Clergymen's daughters did not put their names to works of fiction – not until they were sure they would be successful – and the work was published anonymously as 'By a Lady'. Her publisher, Egerton of Whitehall, had an iniquitous arrangement with her whereby she would have to recompense him for any losses! Fortunately there were no losses. Indeed, she made a personal profit of £140 out of the first edition, which must have been extremely gratifying for her.

The secret of her identity was well kept, even

Below: *Jane enjoyed travelling up to London on the stagecoach to see her publishers and to stay with her easy-going brother Henry, a banker in London at this time.*

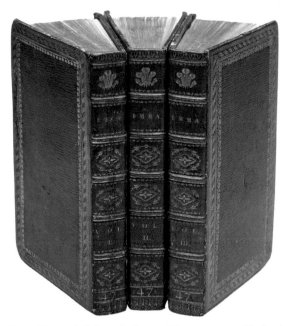

Above: *The specially bound volumes of* Emma, *prepared by Jane's publisher for an admirer of her work, the Prince Regent, later King George IV. They are in the Royal Library at Windsor Castle.*

> *It is a truth universally acknowledged, that a single man in possession of a good fortune, must be in want of a wife.*
>
> PRIDE AND PREJUDICE

It had been written by Jane in an early draft many years before under the title *First Impressions*. She took the phrase 'Pride and Prejudice' from Fanny Burney's *Cecilia*, where in the last chapter it occurs three times. Superbly constructed, *Pride and Prejudice* would become one of the most enjoyable and endlessly re-readable books in the language. Sheridan thought it one of the cleverest things he had ever read. Sir Walter Scott wrote that he had 'read again, for the third time at least, Miss Austen's very finely written novel of Pride and Prejudice', and praised 'her exquisite touch, which renders ordinary and commonplace things and characters interesting from the truth of the description and the sentiment.' The American writer Mark Twain said that whenever he read *Sense and Sensibility* or *Pride and Prejudice* he felt like a bartender who had entered the Kingdom of Heaven.

In Elizabeth Bennet (to whom she may have given much of herself) and in Mr Darcy, Jane

from all those nephews and nieces who so enjoyed Aunt Jane telling them stories. One day Jane and young Anna, one of James's children, were in the circulating library at Alton, looking at the new books just in from London. Jane drew Anna's attention rather casually to a book on display called *Sense and Sensibility*. She watched out of the corners of her eyes as Anna went over to it and picked it up. '*Sense and Sensibility*,' said Anna. 'With a title like that it must be rubbish' and she put it down unopened. But the book did well. Jane's style was lucid, she had momentum, deep feeling, womanliness and wit – there had never before been a writer like her. Her characters were drawn with such clarity and such truth that they were immediately acceptable as counterparts of the men and women of her time and surroundings. She never wrote a cliché or a stale second-hand phrase, and she never wrote a purple passage for cheap effect. Above all, her comedy was a delight, such as when she wrote of Robert Ferrers that he had 'a person and face of strong natural sterling insignificance'.

In 1813 came her second book, which she called *Pride and Prejudice*, and which was to be reprinted within a year. It begins with one of the most often quoted first lines in English literature.

Above: *A portrait of Jane's niece Anna Lefroy, in later life. Anna adored her Aunt Jane and was so saddened when she died that she burnt the manuscript of the novel she was attempting to write.*

Above: *A fashion plate which could well depict Mrs Bennet and two of her daughters in* Pride and Prejudice. *Jane's characters are all so real, and she is a master of the thumbnail sketch.*

Fanny Price – until you get to know them all. And then the timid but courageous Fanny becomes in some respects the most lovable of all Jane's young women. The lowlife scenes in Portsmouth at the end of the book are quite unlike anything else she ever wrote. She was not blind to the sordid underside of life for it is all there in those Portsmouth chapters, with their sense of bugs beneath the wallpaper, of grime between the prongs of the forks.

Round about the second edition of *Mansfield Park* the secret of her identity came out – or rather it was let out by her brother Henry. Although sworn to secrecy, he was proud of her achievement and had been dropping hints wherever he went and whenever he heard people speculating as to who 'the Lady' of the title page might be. Fame did not go to Jane's head: 'What a trifle it all is to the really important points of one's existence.'

Below: *Jane's niece Caroline remembered standing beside her while she played and sang, and thought her voice very sweet.*

created central characters so real that the reader knows them for flesh and blood: Mr and Mrs Bennet, the unspeakably autocratic Lady Catherine de Bourgh, and the egregious Mr Collins, can stand alongside the very finest character drawing of Dickens and Shakespeare. When her brand new copies of *Pride and Prejudice* arrived on the stagecoach from London Jane hurriedly opened the parcel, and then rushed to write in a letter: 'I want to tell you that I have got my own darling child from London.' Her books were surely her children, and all those young heroines she created out of herself were the daughters she never had.

Next came *Mansfield Park*, considered by many to be her masterpiece, a parable of the changes which were slowly beginning to emerge in England. It can be seen as a book about the opposition between potential good and potential evil, and she did not shirk the fact that the good can often seem less attractive than the bad. Thus she makes the scintillating and immoral Henry and Mary Crawford much more interesting, much more likable in many ways, than the heroine

Jane Austen's 6 major novels

Sense and Sensibility	1811
Pride and Prejudice	1813
Mansfield Park	1814
Emma	1816
Northanger Abbey	1818
Persuasion	1818

*J*ane enjoyed the London scene. There were always nephews and nieces up in town, staying at Henry's, to be taken about by her. 'The riding about, the carriage being open was very pleasant. I liked my solitary elegance very much, and was ready to laugh all the time at being where I was. I could not but feel that I had small right to be parading about London in a barouche.' She took the young children to Vauxhall Gardens and on shopping expeditions. She even took them to the dentist while in London – 'which cost us many tears'. Of this London dentist she implied that he was overfond of extracting teeth and money. She enjoyed observing the fashions and the follies of London, and she went to exhibitions of paintings, where it amused her to look for portraits by famous artists which, she felt, just chanced to resemble some of her characters. She seized the opportunity to go to the theatre, hurrying eagerly

Below: *The Exhibition Room, Somerset House. After the death of Eliza, Henry's wife, in 1813, Jane stayed with him and went to several portrait exhibitions.*

Below: *Henry, having taken holy orders, following the collapse in 1816 of the bank in which he had been a partner. Several of his friends lost money in the collapse.*

Above: *The London showrooms of Wedgwood & Byerley. Jane loved visiting the shops in London and a dinner service bought here by Edward can be seen at Chawton.*

to Drury Lane to see the new sensation – the 27-year-old actor Edmund Kean, who, as Shylock, had taken London by storm – and she was most impressed.

On another occasion a party including Jane, Edward, and three of Edward's young daughters, had visited the Lyceum to see *Don Juan – The Libertine Destroyed*, an elaborate production with songs and mime and a spectacular recreation of Hell. During the course of a long day they had travelled all the way from Chawton to stay with Henry, and that evening they all set off for the theatre. Of the archetypal seducer Don Juan, Jane wrote to Cassandra, 'I have seen nobody on the stage who has been a more interesting character than that compound of cruelty and lust.' Concerning another play, she wrote of the actress Miss O'Neill, 'I do not think she was quite equal to my expectations. I fancy I want something more than can be. I took two pocket handkerchiefs, but had very little occasion for either. She is an elegant creature, however, and hugs Mr Young delightfully.'

The Prince Regent, the future King George IV, was extremely unpopular, largely because of his all-too-public humiliation of his rather unsavoury wife, Princess Caroline. Unsavoury or not, Jane took his wife's part. 'Poor woman. I shall support her because she is a woman – and because I hate her husband.' She was working on *Emma* when to her astonishment she received an invitation from the Prince Regent's librarian, the Reverend James Stanier Clarke, to be shown over the Royal residence of Carlton House, a place of fantastic splendour, popularly known as 'Nero's Hotel', because of what was said to go on there!

It was too good an opportunity to miss. She was conducted up the great staircase, through the ornate parade rooms, with footmen in powdered wigs opening the gilded double doors. Halfway through the guided tour, Clarke told her that the Prince Regent was a great admirer of hers, and would be graciously pleased to accept from her the dedication to himself of her next book. There was no gainsaying a Royal command. It was in fact something of an accolade and it would be good for sales. There duly appeared special presentation copies of *Emma* in three volumes, with the Prince of Wales's feathers in gold on the red morocco spine.

Above: *A popular place for entertainment in Jane's day was Vauxhall Gardens, and she took several of her young nephews and nieces to see the attractions there.*

> *Every body allows that the talent of writing agreeable letters is peculiarly female.*
>
> HENRY TILNEY, NORTHANGER ABBEY

*J*ane wrote letters in the same way that many people keep a diary, and they are no less full of rich character sketches than her novels. A number of her letters were destroyed by Cassandra after her death. They must have been revealing letters, written at times of unhappiness and of emotional stress. It is our great good fortune that so many others have survived, full of perceptive observation and amused comment. Those to her niece Fanny Knight are pure gold. She loved Fanny with a protective and maternal tenderness. Advising her on matters of the heart, Jane wrote a succession of letters to her between 1814 and 1817.

'You are the delight of my life … you are worth your weight in gold, or even in the new silver coinage. I cannot express to you what I have felt in reading your history of yourself, how full of Pity and Concern and Admiration and Amusement I have been … you can hardly think what a pleasure it is to me to have such thorough pictures of your Heart.'

'Oh! dear Fanny, your mistake has been one that thousands of women fall into. He was the first young man who attached himself to you. That was the charm, and most powerful it is. Depend upon it, the right man will come at last … who will love you as warmly as ever he did, and who will so completely attach you that you will feel you never really loved before.'

'Nothing can be compared to the misery of being bound without love, bound to one and preferring another.' It is sad to have to record that later in life, as Lady Knatchbull, Fanny behaved very badly towards the memory of her Aunt Jane, writing dismissively of her as lacking in refinement, and 'tainted with common-ness'.

Her niece Anna was by the age of 20 herself showing signs of developing as an author, and was in the process of writing a promising first novel entitled *Enthusiasm*. On receipt of the manuscript, Jane gave her much practical advice and encouragement: 'I am very much obliged to you for sending me your ms. It has entertained me extremely; indeed all of us. I read it aloud to your Grandmama and Aunt Cass, and we were all very much pleased… I shall be very happy to receive more of your work if more is ready.' Of a later chapter she wrote: 'I have read it to your Aunt Cassandra in our room at night while we undressed, with a great deal of pleasure'.

Right: *Jane's 'Dearest Fanny'. She was to Jane 'almost a sister' but in later years Fanny made unkind remarks about her aunt.*

Below: *A needlecase made by Jane for a niece, on display at Chawton. She was very deft with her fingers and made several small items for friends and relations.*

Left: *A Winchester scholar. Jane's nephew James Edward Austen-Leigh, known as Edward, attended the College. In later life he wrote a well-known biography of his famous aunt.*

Above: *Henry wrote to Crosby on Jane's behalf, concealing her identity, to arrange to buy back her manuscript.*

Twelve years had passed since the publisher Crosby had bought *Susan* from Jane for £10. Jane's position was now very different; he had failed to publish the work and she wanted her written pages back. The situation was complicated by the fact that Crosby did not know that this unregarded work, which had been gathering dust in his office for so long, was by the celebrated Jane Austen, for she had conducted all her correspondence with him using a false name. How to recover the work without letting Crosby know he was sitting on a potential money-spinner? Brother Henry came to the rescue and, acting as her agent, he wrote to Crosby offering to buy it back for the same sum the publisher had paid. Both Henry and Jane must have kept their fingers crossed. In due course the manuscript was returned; it was then revised by Jane and subsequently published by John Murray under the title *Northanger Abbey*. Her last completed novel, *Persuasion*, would be published with *Northanger Abbey* after her death.

By the time Jane finished *Persuasion* she was desperately ill, and Henry had gone bankrupt, involving friends and clients in financial disaster. Their uncle, Mr Leigh Perrot, lost £10,000 in the crash. The brothers and sisters shared each others' joys and sorrows, and the strain of Henry's bankruptcy told on them all – and on none more than his ailing sister Jane. She was dying, at the age of only 41, probably of a kidney complaint. When she learned that she had not long to live she made her will, leaving what little she had to Cassandra. It was not very much, for success as an author had come late, and she made at most only £700 from her books in her lifetime. Even so, she left a special bequest of £50 to Henry's elderly housekeeper, who had lost her life's savings in the failure of her employer's bank.

Jane's nephew Edward, the son of her brother James, was a scholar at Winchester School, and spurred on by his aunt's achievements was trying his hand at writing a book. He had written several pages and was very pleased with them but then came disaster. He lost them – they had somehow been thrown away and destroyed. His aunt, on hearing of his misfortune, wrote him a humorous, affectionate, and now very famous letter, commiserating with the young man on his loss, saying she hoped he did not suspect her of secretly purloining them to add them to her latest work. 'But what should I do with your strong manly Vigorous sketches, full of Variety and Glow. How could I possibly join them to the little bit (two inches

Left: *The portrait-sketch of Jane by Cassandra of about 1810. They could never have imagined that one day it would be displayed in the National Portrait Gallery.*

I must not depend upon being ever very blooming again. Sickness is a dangerous indulgence at my time of life.

A LETTER DATED 23 MARCH 1817

wide) of Ivory on which I work with so fine a Brush, as produces little effect after much labour?' She wrote that letter on her last birthday, struggling against the pain and despair of the wretched illness which was killing her.

The last few weeks of her life were spent in Winchester, where she had gone to be near her physician. Close to death, she wrote to Edward again. 'I will not boast of my handwriting; neither that nor my face have yet recovered their proper beauty … God bless you, my dear Edward. If ever you are ill, may you be as tenderly nursed as I have been.' She died in Cassandra's arms on 18 July 1817, and was buried in Winchester Cathedral. In accordance with the custom of the time, the women of the family did not attend the interment; her sister could only stand at the door and watch them take her away.

The author of some of the most enjoyable and endlessly re-readable books in the English language, Jane Austen wrote about the human heart, about envy, pomposity, self-delusion, and about the differences between real love, false love, and self love. There is much more to her than mere sparkle on the surface; there are undercurrents too. Woven into her plots are threads of seduction, illegitimacy, social arrogance, profligacy and betrayal. And she did it all with a glorious instinct for the comedy in the human situation.

Right: *The house in College Street, Winchester, where Jane died on 18 July 1817. The epitaph on her tombstone in Winchester Cathedral reads, in part, as follows:*

THE BENEVOLENCE OF HER HEART, THE SWEETNESS OF HER TEMPER, AND THE EXTRAORDINARY ENDOWMENTS OF HER MIND OBTAINED THE REGARD OF ALL WHO KNEW HER, AND THE WARMEST LOVE OF HER INTIMATE CONNECTIONS.